Bob Willoughby
The
Hollywood Special

A young Audrey Hepburn poses for Paramount Studios photographer Bud Fraker, while two of his assistants hold up the back of her dress as a delicate background. Audrey visited the studio when she was starring in *Gigi* as it toured the country. This was just after she had completed *Roman Holiday* and her first trip to Hollywood. 1953

Bob Willoughby
The
Hollywood Special

Introduction by Tony Curtis

TAKARAJIMA BOOKS

Distributed by D.A.P./

Distributed Art Publishers,

636 Broadway, 12th floor,

New York, NY 10012.

Tel (212) 473-5119,

Fax (212) 673-2887.

Address all other inquiries to

Takarajima Books, Inc.,

200 Varick Street,

New York, NY 10014

Tel (212) 675-1944,

Fax (212) 255-5731.

ISBN 1-883489-03-2

Designed by Tomoyuki Hasumi

and Pamela Virgilio.

Jacket designed by Brian Sisco.

Edited by Kenichiro Tominaga.

Printed and bound in Singapore.

*I*n the grand style, Tony Curtis swashbuckles away as the Great Leslie, dueling the wicked baron, played by Ross Martin. *The Great Race,* Warner Brothers Studios, 1964.

Introduction
by **Tony Curtis**

Lights!

Camera!

Action!

The motion picture camera rolls to tell a story on the screen, utilizing twenty-four frames a second in a carefully lit atmosphere to capture the emotions of a scene—the actors, the light and shadow, the environment, the look envisioned by the director. It is a highly technical moment of celluloid designed to attract the eye of the viewers and involve them in the story.

It is the work of the still photographer, however, to capture the same kind of excitement and emotion in just a single exposure. That is why the art of the still photographer is so demanding—and why the artistry of such masters of the medium as Weegee or Henri Cartier-Bresson has lasted through generations. It takes a great photographer's eye to see that moment and then to capture it. Such is the art of Bob Willoughby, whose collection of photographs here is filled with the essence of motion pictures.

I have had the pleasure of being photographed by Bob Willoughby on many of my films. As an artist since youth myself, I have been able to look at photography with a practiced eye. To create my own drawings, paintings, and time boxes, I have had to recognize structure, appeal, and the relationship of colors, knowing in my mind's eye what the final visual effect will be, just as Bob

Willoughby, when he presses his shutter, has already seen what the photograph will look like. It is an art of the mind that is visual and immediate, and it takes an artist of great stature to achieve that final, visually striking result.

In Billy Wilder's masterpiece, *Sunset Boulevard*, the aging star Norma Desmond said it all about the actors on the screen: "We had faces then." The faces, the close-ups, were there because the photographer knew lighting, the subtlety of shadow, and how all these factors put together would look on film. I have watched Bob Willoughby work with the light that was available to make the faces stand out, to make each photo stand out, to make each photo state a point of view. This is his masterful art, and this is why his work remains as vivid many years later as it did at the moment itself. His work will last because it is a perfect recreation of the mood and the moment and, without twenty-four frames a second, still tells the story.

To capture Bob Willoughby's work in a book is to capture exciting moments of motion picture history that a viewer can look at and study and enjoy over and over again. I am very happy to see Bob's work immortalized in this new and exciting book.

Tony Curtis

*B*ob by Tony on *The Great Race*, Summer '64.

*A*s I was taking the radio receiver off of one of my remote cameras, Tony, seeing the antenna, assumed I was fair game. Undaunted I fought to the bitter end. (As you can see I was also triggering the radio transmitter at my side, hoping that the camera I had mounted on top of the motion picture camera was recording this bloody scene...actor vs. photographer!) *The Great Race,* 1964.

*T*ony, Christine, and Alexandra come for tea. You can see how at ease our boys felt with Tony. (from left) Christopher, David, (Tony) and Stephen Willoughby, and Alexandra Curtis. 1965

*L*ost in a dream of her own, this wistful vision of **Marilyn Monroe** comes closer to what I felt was her real personality rather than her Hollywood image as sex goddess. It touches me every time I see it. Photographed on the 20th Century Fox set of *Let's Make Love,* 1960.

*J*ames Dean seemed to have an instinct for publicity, though I only feel this long after the time. He made friends with several magazine photographers, who carefully documented his young, short life. Yes, he hammed it up, but there was more; he seemed to know what would make a good photograph. The time I visited *Rebel Without a Cause*, he moved away from the set (with me in tow) and sat moodily studying a music score. I don't know if he read music or not, or why the score was there, but this quiet introverted image is one he nurtured to great effect. Warner Brothers Studios, 1955.

*E*ver the watcher, **James Dean** sits in the shadows between takes, studying everyone. I never had the opportunity to work with him on a film, so it is hard to know if he really was a moody character or if it was just another act, like his imitation of Brando I used to see him do around town. Whatever the truth, when *Rebel* was released he became an instant star; the year was 1955.

*D*ear Audrey. When I took this photograph in her hotel room in Los Angeles, how could I know I would work on so many films with her, what a success she would become, what a friend. **Audrey Hepburn** crossed my path for the first time in 1953 and this first portrait I made of her is still one of my favorites.

*S*itting alone on the Warner Brothers sound stage, **Audrey Hepburn** waits for rehearsals on *My Fair Lady* to begin. Soon, on these same stairs, through the magic of film, she would be transformed into a princess going to the ball, or so the story goes. The real problem was keeping the princess from showing through the makeup of the urchin Eliza early in the film. 1963

*B*alefully glaring through cigarette smoke, **Peter O'Toole** poses for an early morning portrait at the Beverly Hills Hotel. This was his first Hollywood visit after his acclaimed performance in *Lawrence of Arabia*. 1962

*E*lizabeth **Taylor** shocked her fans when she gained so much weight for the Warner film *Who's Afraid of Virginia Woolf?* Playing the blousy, vitriolic Martha, she turned in an Academy Award-winning performance under the direction of Mike Nichols. 1965

*C*omic **Danny Kaye** gallops and glides his way in a modern dance number in Paramount's *White Christmas*. I was with him one afternoon when he spoke in his French double-talk to a visitor from Paris. "I know he's speaking French, but I can't understand him," she confided to me. He had a fantastic ear for sound, for the rhythm of speech. 1953

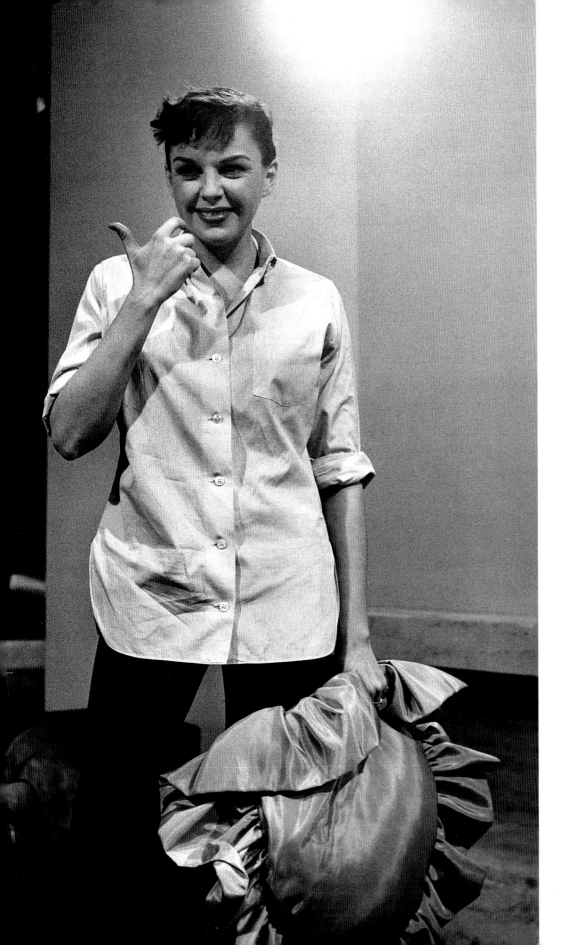

*L*aughing at the end of a strenuous scene, **Judy Garland** pauses to catch her breath on the set of *A Star Is Born*. Warner's publicity department had been so afraid that I would upset this temperamental star, they had me hiding behind studio lights to get my first pictures. 1954

*F*red **Astaire** talks to his stunt double on the night location of Columbia's *Notorious Landlady.* I remember it as a very cold night, and the setting up seemed to take even longer than usual. I was walking past one of the little wooden cubicles on wheels they call dressing rooms, and was amazed by the sound of tapping as fast as an automatic weapon. It turned out to be Fred trying to keep warm in his own way.

1961

*T*here was an Apache dance sequence in the film *Can Can*, and the choreographer wisely thought to provide a dummy for **Shirley MacLaine** for the classic pounding the woman takes in the dance. When I asked her to pose next to it, everyone had a great laugh. 20th Century Fox Studios, 1959.

This aspect of **Richard Attenborough** is totally atypical. A bundle of enthusiastic energy, he jumps into his roles with passion. Here on the location of *Doctor Dolittle*, he recharges his batteries. Three years later in London, I was walking backwards photographing Christopher Jones and his agents for *Life*, when I heard a screech of brakes. I turned to see a man leap out of a Rolls Royce heading right for me with open arms. I tried to get out of the way of this guided missile but was spun around with cameras flying. He said something about how good it was to see me, and in a wink he was gone. We all stood open-mouthed at this apparition. It was Richard just saying hello. 1966

Anita Ekberg, a long-legged, statuesque blond from Malmö, Sweden, here on Paramount Studio's set of *Artists & Models*, didn't really find her place in Hollywood as well as she did in Italy. In *La Dolce Vita*, four years later, she made her mark in film lore. 1955

*T*he film *Susan Slept Here* gave me the first chance to work with **Debbie Reynolds**. I was quite unprepared for her wonderfully spontaneous humor, and it was a treat. Here she tries to convince one of the crew members (who must polish the floor before the next take) to dance with her. He tries to work around her, but she is determined . . .

*N*o matter which way he went Debbie was there. He didn't have a chance. He forgot the floor and went into a time step...so who says dance lessons aren't worthwhile? Debbie has her way! RKO Studios, 1954.

*M*arlon **Brando** "sings and dances," proclaimed the various papers. I was assigned by *This Week* magazine to cover just that. What a departure from the image of the mumbling character he had played in so many films. Here you see Broadway choreographer **Michael Kidd** putting Brando through his paces. Marlon's physical ability and agility amazed Kidd, and they got on famously during the rehearsals for Damon Runyon's popular musical, *Guys & Dolls*. Goldwyn Studios, 1955.

*R*ehearsals for *South Pacific* were going on over at Fox Studios, and I was assigned by *This Week* magazine to cover it. **Mitzi Gaynor**, who is terrific to work with, was rehearsing the *Honey Bun* number when director **Josh Logan** arrived. He heard the music, and like a fighter entering the ring, stepped right into the number, causing Mitzi to fall apart laughing. Josh had seen the number so often when he directed the Broadway show, he knew every step by heart! 1957

*D*oris Day stands in the doorway of her Universal Studios dressing room surrounded by all of her ladies-in-waiting: makeup, hairdressing, wardrobe, etc. A really fine singer, with a personality that made the crew very relaxed around her. In the adjoining dressing room, **Rex Harrison** (you can just see his feet on a stool inside) relaxes while his sole dresser sits outside and reads. *Midnight Lace*, 1960.

$\mathcal{M}$ontgomery **Clift** was called to the makeup room at MGM Studios for tests to see what kind of mustache and beard would suit him best for his role in *Raintree County*. His co-star and friend **Elizabeth Taylor** accompanied him, but so monopolized the mirror that it was almost impossible for the makeup crew to do their job. 1956

I always found this photograph of **Olivia De Havilland** more than a little interesting, for the reflection in the mirror looks like her sister Joan Fontaine, with whom there was always a rivalry. Joan got the first Academy Award between them. Even here, her sister seems to haunt her. My favorite image of Olivia was as Maid Marion in *Robin Hood.* When I saw the film as a youth, I was smitten. When *Glamour* assigned me to do a story on Hollywood blonds, I was delighted to finally meet the lady who rang my bell so many years before. 1954

*C*harles **Boyer** peering into his dressing-room mirror at the old Selznick Studios still appears the romantic leading man. In the 30s and 40s he played opposite all the most famous female stars. Here doing a series at Four-Star Studios, which he helped found, he gives the ladies in *Glamour* another dose of his Gallic charm. 1953

*N*atalie Wood had been in films since she was a child, but no one could have imagined she would develop into such a beauty. Here, delicious in her costume for *The Great Race*, she listens to director Blake Edwards as they rehearse. Warner Brothers Studios, 1964.

*I*t just goes to prove one thing: **Jane Fonda** can look pretty terrific no matter where she lays her lovely body down. This photograph was made on the New York City location of *Klute*, in a tacky dressmaking loft. Jane was waiting for production to start when I saw her sitting in the shadows across the room. 1970

*P*aramount Studios famed costume designer **Edith Head** (like so many men before her) studies the generous proportions of **Sophia Loren**, trying to decide what would suit her best for her role in *Black Orchid*. 1958

*L*ovely young **Jean Seberg**, on location in La Lavandu in the south of France, waits for shooting to begin on *Bonjour Tristesse*. Her second film with Otto Preminger had not yet changed this optimistic teenager. Full of life, smiling, laughing, mostly at her own mistakes, she was a delight to the cast and crew. 1957

*T*his photograph was taken in Provence, France, on the location of *The Lion in Winter*. The production team constantly guessed wrong, scheduling all of the interior shots on sunny days, and all of the exterior shots on days with so much rain that the sets for the barge landing bringing Eleanor of Aquitaine to Henry were flooded. **Katharine Hepburn** seeks shelter next to the camera on one such wet day. Behind her **Anthony Hopkins** and **Peter O'Toole** prepare for the next scene...come rain or shine! 1967

Mia **Farrow**, free spirit, was a happy force on this downbeat film. *Rosemary's Baby* was not a laugh a minute, but Mia kept things popping. Here you see her Indian-wrestling with one of the grips on the Paramount set. The idea is to knock your opponent off balance, and when Mia actually beat this strong crewman, much to the delight of his buddies, he was kidded for days. 1967

*B*rigadoon was a wonderful Broadway show. Agnes DeMille's choreography revolutionized dance in American theater and now it was to be transformed into a film. MGM assigned their two creative masters, director **Vincent Minelli** and dancer-choreographer **Gene Kelly**, to the task. Here Kelly shows Minelli the movement of the dancers as stillsman **Eric Carpenter** shoots a 3D photo for Minelli to study. 1954

I was in Arizona covering the location filming of *Oklahoma* for *The New York Times,* when I received a request from Warner Brothers to fly back to Los Angeles and photograph an added musical production number on *A Star Is Born.* **Judy Garland** is seen here rehearsing in her makeup smock and slippers. Choreographer **Richard Barstow** watches intently (background right). On this film I had my first *Life* cover. 1954

*N*ight shooting on the 20th Century Fox Studios set of *Can Can* and **Frank Sinatra** seen here giving out to producer **Jack Cummings** about the delay in production. Frank, never one to show much patience with such things, had to be reassured often. "Stroking," they call it now, but then it only meant ulcers for Jack. 1959

As director **Otto Preminger** complains to the actors, **Frank Sinatra** withdraws from the firing line to memorize the script changes on *The Man* *with the Golden Arm.* This was the first time the problem of drug addiction had been trotted out for the movie-going public. 1955

*O*tto **Preminger**, always a controversial director, seemed to make it his profession to flaunt the Legion of Decency guidelines—this time with the taboo subject of drug addiction. Seen here with a new and nervous **Kim Novak**, he patiently explains her role. RKO Studios, 1955.

*D*irector **Blake Edwards** scores a direct hit on **Natalie Wood**. Part of the big pie fight sequence on the film *The Great Race* which took five days to shoot. An already pie-covered **Jack Lemmon** leans over to watch Natalie get hers. Cinematographer **Russ Harlen** keeps an eye out from above. Several days earlier he literally saved my life, moving me and my camera from a spot where, seconds later, a trick car driven by Peter Falk crashed. Over the movie camera's matte box is mounted my still camera with a radio receiver attached. So, as I shot this picture of Blake throwing the pie, I caught a close-up of the pie hitting Natalie. During filming, I often had three cameras in different locations being triggered. Warner Brothers Studios, 1954.

I think **John Wayne** actually invented the movie fight style. Designed for the camera, the blows seem to hit, when really they just miss the face (when everything goes to plan). Here rehearsing with bad man **Bruce Dern**, Wayne choreographs the fight for director **Mark Rydell** (far right) and cinematographer **Bob Surtees** (with glasses) at Warner Brothers Studios during the filming of *The Cowboys*. 1971

*R*ex **Harrison** seems to be enjoying the story that composer **Leslie Bricusse** is telling him. Rex was waiting his turn in the makeup room on the 20th Century Fox film of *Doctor Dolittle*. Reflected in the mirror are two young actors waiting to get Rex's autograph. 1966

*C*hecking his lines with script supervisor **Meta Rebner**, **Dustin Hoffman** prepares for the next scene in *The Graduate*. When we were first introduced, I asked him if he was called "Dusty," and he gave me a strange look. "Your mother is Lillian and your father is Harry and you have a brother named Ronald?" "OK, OK. How do you know all of this?" I told him that when he was a baby, I used to live upstairs in the same house on Orange Drive and I was his babysitter. What a small world! 1967

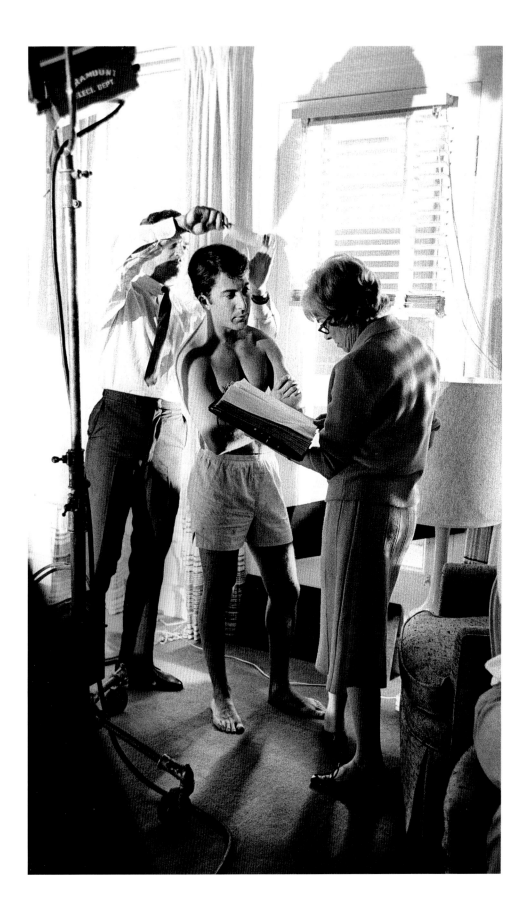

*I*was assigned to photograph the screen test of a lovely young New York model, **Margo McKendry**, for *Show* magazine at Universal Studios. We had just broken for lunch and I was sitting with director George England, his assistant, and **John Saxton**, who was doing the test with Margo. I was amazed at the number of men who, spotting Margo, found some reason to visit our table. Howard Keel held forth for a while until he was replaced by **Cary Grant**. He offered to help her with her lines later...and who could refuse? Alas, Margo wasn't signed. 1961

*J*udy Garland, ready to go on stage for her TV special, scoops up her lovely little daughter, **Lorna Luft**, who with her sister Liza, had come to see Mom at work. 1955

Lorna, imitating mother, had dancing in her genes. Seen here at CBS-TV Center in Los Angeles, she looks ready to go on stage herself. This set of pictures was submitted to *Life* magazine where a sub picture editor had tossed them in the reject pile when the publisher just happened to pass by. As the story goes, the publisher retrieved them and the photos ran in the next issue. Later *Life* used this photo in their full-page newspaper ads across the country, as proof that *Life* brings important photographs to their readers every week—as long as the publisher keeps his eyes open.

*L*orna **Luft**, with her sister **Liza Minelli**. Backstage was home and stepping over cables an everyday event. CBS-TV Center, Los Angeles, 1955.

Mickey Rooney almost cut his teeth on this lot. I'm sure he knew every foot of ground...backwards. When his son, **Teddy**, visited him, he gave him a lesson in publicity photography. MGM Studios, 1958.

*E*ye to eye, this little fan takes the measure of his cowboy hero **John Wayne**. Duke, as everyone called him, was crusty, but having young children of his own gave him a gentle response to the younger members of the cast on *The Cowboys*. Seen here on both the New Mexico and Colorado locations of the Warner Brothers film. 1971

Young **Kate Burton** pleads with her father, **Richard Burton**, to let her try her hand at fishing. Typically, Richard says nothing, but all along is just baiting the hook for his daughter. One of the rare moments away from the film set when they could have a moment together. On location of *Who's Afraid of Virginia Woolf?* in Northhampton, Massachusetts. 1965

*S*ome days things just fall into place, like this totally spontaneous dance sequence with **Lauren Bacall** and her daughter **Leslie Bogart**. I had been at their home doing color portraits of Lauren, and then with the children. A lovely day in Beverly Hills and right in front of me this little ballet emerged. Luckily my camera was still loaded. Probably the most charming moments of the entire day's shooting was captured. 1958

*L*ittle **Sachi Parker** visiting the 20th Century Fox set of *Can Can*, tells her friends, "That's my Mommy!" As reflected in the mirror, the cast and crew are working on the dream sequence of *The Garden of Eden*.

Mommy, **Shirley MacLaine**, dressed as Eve, comes over to see how **Sachi** is doing, teaching her to stick out her tongue. Sachi was always called Skoshi at this time; the Japanese word for "little". 1959

*L*iv Ullmann enjoys her little daughter's reaction to her being dressed in such "funny" clothes. **Linn** had flown all the way from Sweden to be with her mother on the Big Sur location of *Zandy's Bride*. 1973

A lovely moment at home with **Tony Curtis** and his beautiful young bride, **Christine Kaufmann**, with their new baby daughter **Alexandra**. Tony was an avid photographer and a very good painter, and at this time was working on little boxes like the ones by Joseph Cornell. Beverly Hills, 1964.

*T*ony **Perkins**, when working in Rome on *This Angry Age*, became the crush of the daughter of his co-star, Silvana Mangano. Little **Rafaella de Laurentis**, now a producer like her father, was wishing she was 20 years older. 1958

*S*ilvana **Mangano** caresses **Tony Perkins**' hair much to the annoyance of little **Rafaella**, who jealously pretends she doesn't care. 1958

*T*his little chimpanzee was doing a TV show on the Columbia Studios lot when spotted having a walk with its trainer by animal lover, **Kim Novak**. Kim was working on *Notorious Landlady* at the time and having a long time romance with its director, Richard Quine. 1961

Long before the filming of *Green Mansions* began, **Audrey Hepburn** was given this young fawn to live with, literally, so that it would be comfortable around her during the making of the film.

1958

*A*udrey took little "Ip" everywhere she went, even
shopping in Beverly Hills.
Ip was a real attention
getter. People would stop
work to come over and
see it, and in a town
noted for being blasé,
this was an accomplish-
ment. To Ip, Audrey was
a mother figure and Ip
followed her everywhere,
much to the annoyance
of Audrey's dog, Famous,
who gave the deer a
wide berth. 1958

Mary Pickford, once "America's sweetheart," gave a party at her famous home, Pickfair, and invited all of the silent movie stars. I was covering it for *Life* magazine. The silent comedian **Harold Lloyd**, says good-bye to Mary. In the background, a painting of Mary as she was remembered in her silent films. 1956

*L*illian Gish, the first lady of the silent screen, pours tea at Pickfair. Both she and her sister Dorothy appeared in some of the most notable silent films of the time. Lillian also worked on the stage, playing at one time Ophelia against John Gielgud's Hamlet. 1956

*N*o film buff would have a problem identifying these two wonderful faces: **Buster Keaton** and **Joe E. Browne** clowning for my camera at the Pickfair party. I never thought I would have the opportunity to photograph these great comedians. I once watched Keaton and Chaplin rehearse a number during the filming of *Limelight,* but at that time I was only allowed to photograph Claire Bloom, as W. Eugene Smith had a photographic exclusive for *Life*. 1956

Gary **Cooper** in black tie enjoying the "El Dorado" party at the Ambassador Hotel in Los Angeles. It was Dorothy Chandler's bash to raise money for the LA Music Center.

Before I left Los Angeles, I photographed the opening of that center for *Vogue* magazine, so I was able to see the positive results of the many fund-raisers. 1955

*T*he Factory, the "in" place in Hollywood at the time, was hosting a big charity night. I was covering it for *Look* magazine. The problem was, no flash and light levels down to zero. I had been experi-menting with a new film used originally for the army with a 3200 ASA. We found we could push it one stop to 6400, but since red hurricane lamps were the main light source and this film was color blind to reds, well, I could only hope for the best. **Ava Gardner** had always been one of my dream women when I was a young man, but I never had the opportunity of working with her. On this night she was there with famous hair stylist **Sydney Guilaroff** whom I had known for years at MGM and he introduced us. I felt like a fan myself as I gurgled my delight. 1967

*D*ominic Dunne, then a producer at 20th Century Fox, and his lovely wife Linnie were having one of their famous parties and *Vogue* magazine asked me to cover it. It was filled with celebrities, but the unlikely combination of **Tuesday Weld** and **Truman Capote** held me enthralled. Tuesday is telling me to put down the camera and come dance with them. That would have been something indeed! 1964

*F*rank **Sinatra** and his rat pack were filming *Oceans 11* during the day and playing at the Sands Hotel at night. Where they got the energy, I do not know. But energy they had. At night they played off each other, working out new ploys to break each other up...one trying to top the other. **Dean Martin**, **Sammy Davis, Jr.**, **Peter Lawford**, **Joey Bishop**, and **Buddy Lester**. Las Vegas, 1960.

*F*rank **Sinatra** rehearsing for his nightly show at the Sands Hotel. I've watched him over the years on stage and in the studio, and the place he is most relaxed is in the recording studio, or at a moment like this. No pressure, doing what he did best. He had a totally different and more gentle personality. Las Vegas, 1960.

*T*he stage across from the one I was working on at MGM opened its doors for lunch, and I heard the unmistakable sound of **Louis Armstrong**'s trumpet. I grabbed my camera and snapped this noon-time jam session for the cast and crew. In the background, leaning against the piano, is director **Chuck Walters**, **Grace Kelly**, and **Bing Crosby**. *High Society*, 1956.

*T*alented pianist **Jack Lemmon** relaxes between shots on *Notorious Landlady*, watched by his good friend and director **Richard Quine**. Quine, also adept on the 78, made sure a piano was always on the set. Columbia Studios, 1961.

*J*ames **Stewart** was James Stewart on or off the screen. I worked with him several times after *The Glenn Miller Story* and he was always the charming, slow-speaking character he portrayed on the screen. A real gentleman and always a pleasure to work with. Universal Studios, 1953.

*D*anny Kaye incomparable.
Off screen in rehearsals
he was a tear-away.
His director once told me
that they wished they

could get that kind of spontaneity on screen. Here, during rehearsals at the Hollywood Bowl, he takes over Meredith Wilson's orchestra...too fast, too slow, until everyone falls about and they have to declare a recess. 1954

Alfred **Hitchcock** always made his presence felt— his imagination, his description of a scene so clear that even non-actors became involved in the images he conjured up. Here, **Tippi Hedren** is mesmerized by the director, on the Universal Studios set of *Marnie*. One of my greatest plea- sures was having him sit me down and tell me the entire film as he envision- ed it. The actual shooting of the film, to him, was an anti-climax. 1964

*B*urt Lancaster listens...
but is he convinced about
what director **Fred
Zinnemann** is telling him
for the fight scene
between Sinatra and
Ernest Borgnine? A
perfectionist, Zinnemann
drives home his argument
on the Columbia Studios
set of *From Here to
Eternity.* 1953

Warner Brothers gave me their script for *Petulia* and I went to the San Francisco location to see what I could pick up. It was quickly obvious that director **Richard Lester** was working with a different script than anyone else. Lester, the whiz kid who did the fun Beatles films, worked with multiple cameras on most of scenes, picking up various details. I once heard George C. Scott remark after one take that he didn't know what the cameras were shooting! Here, Lester tries to rev-up actress **Julie Christie** for the coming scene. 1967

When **Jean Seberg** won the title role in the film *Saint Joan*, director **Otto Preminger** promised her a dream trip to Paris as a special prize, including a chance to see **Ingrid Bergman** in *Tea and Sympathy*. After the performance Otto took Jean backstage and introduced the newest Joan to Ingrid, who had played the same role eight years earlier. Jean was noticeably awed to be with such a famous actress. Ingrid was reassuring and commented that "each time they make this film, the hair seems to get shorter!"

1956

*J*ames **Dean** was working across the street on another sound stage at Warner Brothers Studio. My agent called to tell me they had a fan magazine assignmment on him and I should go over when I had a break and get a few shots. "It's just a little film," I was told—*Rebel Without a Cause*! When I did get over, director **Nicholas Ray** was conferring with Dean, and I took a few shots, never guessing this "little film" would achieve cult status. 1955

A young **Natalie Wood** listens to director **Nicholas Ray** on the darkened set of *Rebel Without a Cause*. Ray made a habit, I noticed, of getting his actors away from the set and quietly preparing them for the coming dramatic scenes. 1955

We all have different
ideas about what made
Marilyn Monroe so
special. That innocent
sexuality was legend.
Here on the set of *Let's*
Make Love, she turns
the laser-beam of her
attention onto the camera
operator, who is hapless
and willing. 20th Century
Fox Studios, 1960.

*S*ometimes one finds more drama off the set than on. My assignment for *American Weekly* was to show the men in **Marilyn Monroe**'s life. At the side of the stage, a heated discussion was going on between Marilyn and co-star **Yves Montand**, while her husband **Arthur Miller** listened passively. *Let's Make Love*, Fox Studios, 1960.

*N*o matter that she was the most famous actress at the time, **Elizabeth Taylor** still looks star struck, touching her hair nervously, when she meets the legendary **Marlene Dietrich** on the Warner Brothers set of *Who's Afraid of Virginia Woolf?* 1965

*P*ut irrepressible **Jack Lemmon** head to head with **William Holden** and the sparks are bound to fly. Jack was on his honeymoon in Paris and decided to stir things up, here visiting the set of *Paris When It Sizzles* at the Boulogne Studios, where Bill was working with Audrey Hepburn. 1962

*B*ob **Hope** visits fellow comedian **Danny Kaye** on the set of *Knock on Wood*. Not to trade jokes, but to discuss their golf game, and that was serious stuff. Paramount Studios, 1955.

*F*ather and daughter meet in a make-believe world. **Henry Fonda** comes over from the adjoining sound stage to visit with his tired daughter **Jane**, who was working on *They Shoot Horses, Don't They?* The Fonda dynasty of actors continues to this day. Warner Brothers Studios, 1969.

*F*amous French film actress **Simone Signoret** visits the set of *They Shoot Horses, Don't They?* and chats with director **Sidney Pollock**. Seated, to the right, is actor **Michael Conrad**, welcoming the break. This surely was the most physically exhausting film for actors that I have ever worked on. Warner Brothers Studios, 1969.

Orson **Welles** was the center of attraction this day in Guymas, Mexico, where he was filming *Catch 22*. It wasn't the film crew at work, but two visitors doing other than what they were more famous for. Actress **Candice Bergen**, photographing Orson being interviewed by film director **Peter Bogdanovich**. Welles was always one of my film heroes. When I was attending the USC film school, I remember seeing *Citizen Kane* about 30 times! On the Guymas location, I found myself sitting alone with him and eager to know more about the film from the master. I blew the whole thing by opening with, "I suppose you're bored talking about *Citizen Kane*." "Yes, I am," was his response, and that was the end of that! 1969

*F*amily reunion time as **Warren Beatty** visits his sister **Shirley MacLaine** on the 20th Century Fox set of *Can Can*. Warren always seemed to be with a different lady; this day it was **Joan Collins**. I worked with Shirley many times, but this was the only time I saw her with her brother. 1959

Who would recognize
Yul Brynner with hair?
Here **Charlton Heston**
and his son stop to
challenge this familiar
face to "come out from
under the rug." At the
time, they were both
working on the ill-fated
film, *The Buccaneer*,
at Paramount Studios.
Brynner's bike was
inscribed with "Rhymes
with Sinner," and his
office was filled with
African weapons and
whips. Macho time in
the old corral? 1958

I was with **Sophia Loren** in the Paramount Studios commissary where we were going to have lunch and suddenly she was on her feet as she had spied **Elvis Presley** walking through. I don't think she had ever met him, but Italian enthusiasm cannot be denied. In a minute she was sitting on his lap, tousling his hair, all to his great discomfort. He was also aware that I was taking his picture, so what could he do? What could any man do... surrender! The skirmish was over as quickly as it had begun. She was only saying how much she liked his music. 1958

As **Jack Lemmon**'s character in the film *Luv* is about to jump off the Brooklyn Bridge, he is greeted by an old school chum, played by **Peter Falk**. Jack and Peter really were old chums, having worked together several years earlier on *The Great Race*. The Manhattan skyline in the background...and yes there is a platform just below Jack in case he slipped. 1966

*T*aking a break between shots on the Universal Studios set of *Marnie*, **Sean Connery** talks with actress **Louise Latham**. I worked briefly on this film for *Life* magazine. About two years later I was walking down the street at another studio when Sean stopped and called my name. With so many crews and photographers that he must have encountered in that period, I was flattered. 1964

*C*ornwall, England.
It's cold and wet and the
weather is holding up
filming on the UK
location of *Summer*

Flight. **Susan Hayward**
braves it out amidst the
glamour of a Fowey
garage cum makeup
room. 1962

I was having lunch with **Jennifer Jones** at the 20th Century Fox commissary and we were having a great conversation. We walked back to the set of *Tender Is the Night* and she literally became a different person. I was a photographer then and to be avoided at all costs, or so it would seem. It became an impossible assignment. This photograph was made in near darkness, at the very back of the soundstage where she hid between shots.

1961

One always hears about the glamour of films. The reality of sets filled with props, electrical clutter, cut off from the sun, hours of waiting, is quite another thing. **Nancy Kwan**, dressed in her costume for *Flower Drum Song*, sits amidst the detritus of the Universal set waiting for the assistant director to come and nudge her back into action. 1961

*B*eautiful young Italian actress **Pier Angeli** was brought to Hollywood after her acclaimed portrayal of a sensitive young girl in *Theresa*. MGM cast her as a circus performer, and she spent months learning to work on a trapeze. Seen here with co-star **Kirk Douglas** as they listen to director **Gottfried Reinhardt**, when they were doing the "Equilibrium" segment in *The Story of Three Loves*. 1952

Steve **McQueen** leaning up against a horse on the Prescott, Arizona, location of *Junior Bonner*. It reminds me of the character he played on the TV series, *Wanted: Dead or Alive,* when it was apparent that McQueen had a unique screen presence. "I would like to put money on him," I remember saying. On the few days that I photographed him, he was hard to pin down. When he wasn't filming he was either holed up in his dressing room or off across the desert on his motorcycle.

1971

*O*ut of the heat of the
lights, **Kirk Douglas**
watches preparations for
the coming scene of
The Juggler. Kirk had
an intensive six-week
course in juggling to be
able to shoot all of the
scenes without a real
juggler doubling for him.
Columbia Studios,
1952.

*F*or my money **Robert Mitchum** is one of the best actors in Hollywood. For years he made scripts come alive, even when they were badly written. Bogart had that capacity too—to be believable. Here in a scene from *Cape Fear*, Bob plays the heavy once again. Universal Studios, 1961.

*H*arper's *Bazaar* assigned me to photograph two new young actors who were appearing in MGM's *The Cobweb*. **John Kerr** and **Susan Strasberg**, fresh from Broadway. Susan is the daughter of Lee Strasberg, founder of the Actors Studios in New York City. 1955

Locationing down the
coast towards Malibu,
Gregory Peck and
Deborah Kerr relax as
they wait for the cameras
to roll on Fox's epic *The
Beloved Infidel*. Peck
played the writer F. Scott
Fitzgerald during his
tumultuous affair with
columnist Sheila Graham.
It was always a pleasure
to work with such
professional actors as
Peck and Kerr. 1959

*T*wo pretty girls sharing a secret and a hat. **Jean Seberg** and **Mylène Demongeot** on the Riviera location of *Bonjour Tristesse*. At the time, each had a young lover who would appear at breakfast in total collapse, while Jean and Mylène bounced down the stairs two at a time. La Lavandu, 1957.

*A*uthoress **Françoise Sagan** talks to **David Niven** on the location filming of her novel, *Bonjour Tristesse*. Background left: **Deborah Kerr**. La Lavandu, 1957.

*V*isiting **Vivien Leigh** enjoys **Deborah Kerr** describing her first water skiing experience on the location of *Bonjour Tristesse*. Two beautiful English roses in the south of France. 1957

*D*uring the filming of *Raintree County*, **Montgomery Clift** had a tragic car accident after leaving a party at Elizabeth's late one night. He had plastic surgery and MGM shut the film down until he recovered, but his face and personality were never the same again. Here on location in Danville, Kentucky, **Elizabeth Taylor** indulges Monty in his pranks. I know she felt desperately sorry for him. The studio doctor told me that Monty had more medicine in his bag than he had in his. 1956

*G*rado in the north of Italy was the location for *A Farewell to Arms*. **Rock Hudson** opens the curtains to get some light in his little portable dressing room and finds Italian ladies of all ages eager to get a look at the Hollywood star. I was covering Rock on assignment for *Look* magazine and it was almost impossible to go anywhere without a crowd forming. 1957

*A*s unlikely an image
of screen tough-guy
Humphrey Bogart as
one would ever see.
Here holding his
children's party favors,
at Liza Minelli's sixth
birthday party held at
Ira Gershwin's home in
Beverly Hills. 1952

Afterword
by **Bob Willoughby**

To work on a film set, you absolutely had to be a member of the union. This was a completely closed shop; only members and their children were allowed in the door. Outside photographers were allowed in to cover special sequences on a film, but only rarely. When they were, the studios were obliged to pay the unions what was known as a "stand-by" fee for every day the non-union photographer spent on the set. The money was put aside for the union's welfare fund.

Life and *Look* magazines were courted by all of the studios. Their circulation, which was in the millions, was a direct conduit to the movie-going public. It was editorial space the studios could never buy.

The magazines, at the height of their prestige, might ask the studios for an exclusive from one of the scenes in a particular film. That meant no other magazine could use similar material, and the studio's publicity department would have to put a hold on all of its own photographic art from that sequence.

As it frequently turned out, if the magazine's film critic didn't like the film when it was previewed, the magazine wouldn't run the exclusive, leaving the studio without any publicity on one of the most important and often most marketable scenes. On the other hand, if the exclusive did run, the box-office rewards were significant enough to make the studio feel the risk was worth taking.

The smaller circulation magazines were welcomed, but rarely got onto the studio lots for very long. I would be assigned to photograph an actor, and maybe I would get some shots in his dressing room or around a set that wasn't being filmed. The publicity men were warm, but they had to function under rules from the head office: Do not hold up production, and do not distract the actors or directors. So generally it was in one door and out the other before you knew it. A nice lunch in the studio commissary, a warm handshake, and that was it.

When I came to Warner Brothers with six or seven important assignments on *A Star Is Born*, starring Judy Garland, I was given the unique opportunity to work on a set over a period of several days.

As I watched the film crew, I realized how they worked together as a unit. This was not at first evident to me, but the longer I was there, the more I could observe a rhythm in the way they went about their various tasks. This rhythm was usually created by a good assistant director who kept things moving.

After several years of experience, it was clear how an outside photographer—or anyone who came in to work for just a few hours—stood out. Not that they were necessarily in the way, but they did not move with the crew. And working with the crew was imperative. When that camera moved on a

I had just returned from assignments in India and several other countries, when MGM asked me to cover their production of William Henry Hudson's famous novel, *Green Mansions*. The best treat of all—Audrey Hepburn was to play Rima, the bird girl. Originally planned for filming in the Venezuelan jungle, it was finally decided to recreate a jungle on their largest sound stage. What a wonderful moment each morning, to step into this moist garden they had populated with exotic plants and animals...out of the Californian sun,

dolly, I had to know where everyone was going to be, where the sound man was going to move with his boom. The lights, the props that moved. Where the script supervisor needed to be to watch the actor's movements. This is not to forget the actors and director who are concentrating totally... a click at the wrong moment! Disaster.

It was good schooling, and over the years, no matter which country we were in, I found that it was much the same. The crews were all professional, generally knew each other, and had worked together before. It was their rhythm I had to get into. Sometimes that was easy, sometimes it meant learning a new way. It could take me several days before I could function well on a new set.

After viewing Cukor's final cut on *A Star Is Born*, Warner Brothers executives decided that they needed something more. They brought in a big production number, I think from MGM. It was the *Born in a Trunk* sequence, and they asked me to come back and cover it for the magazines. They were willing to pay me.

This was quite amazing. As far as I know it was the first time that any studio had ever done this. It was extraordinary! It meant, as I said earlier, that the studio would have to pay double—my fee to me *and* the standby fee to the union.

This gamble was to pay off on *Lose That Face*. I had my first *Life* cover, and I was able to break into and concrete sound stages, into the set with all the smells and sounds of a tropical rain forest! I had the idea of photographing Audrey as Rima using a defraction grating I had made. Rima was supposed to be a magic spirit, and I strived to get this mystic feeling in all of my close-ups. When I showed the results to Audrey and Mel Ferrer (both Audrey's husband, and the film's director), they told me that this was the very look they had hoped for. They showed the pictures to Joe Ruttenberg, who was one of MGM's most famous cinematographers, and told him that this was the way they wanted all of Audrey's close-ups reshot! I was terribly embarrassed ... Joe had five Academy Awards to his credit, and I did not wish to offend him. He was wonderful, of course, throughout the filming, and ever ready to hold a light when I needed a special photograph. The film was not critically acclaimed, to say the least, but I got great space in the various magazines with my material. And working with Audrey and Tony, a very great pleasure. 1958

Photo: Eric Carpenter

several other magazines. This was what made the Warner Brothers publicity department realize that, by hiring me to cover their big scenes, even if *Life* didn't use the spread, I could easily trot it over to *Look* or to *Collier's* or to one of the other magazines I was already working for.

And that's how I became the "special." It started a whole career for me. This of course didn't happen overnight, but it was in 1954 that it all began to come together.

In 1956, George Nichols telephoned me from MGM, telling me that they had a new film they hoped would be another *Gone with the Wind* ... and would I be interested in covering it for about three months?

Well, a free-lancer in Los Angeles had to be willing to do everything, and if one got an assignment for one full day, one was clicking one's heels in delight. This was for three months! I was flabbergasted. I don't know what I said, but he got the idea that it was OK with me. I told him my daily fee, which he upped, saying that he wanted to keep me happy. And then he told me something I'd never forget.

He had gone to New York to poll the magazine editors about who they wanted to have cover *Raintree County*, this major film epic starring Montgomery Clift and Elizabeth Taylor. He said that without exception every one of the editors he

*I*n 1952 I had already started to work for *Harper's Bazaar*. So when my agent rang about the photo call on Marilyn Monroe, he had to remind me that while I worked for some upmarket magazines, I was also poor, and "anything you can get on Marilyn will sell." With this logic ringing in my ears, I went off to discover that every other photographer in town had been told the same thing. The event was to introduce the song "Marilyn," which orchestra leader Ray Anthony had written in

spoke with mentioned my name.

As a learning tool, old magazines were ideal, and the secondhand magazine shops (I don't know if anything like this exists anymore) became my home away from home. There were several in Hollywood, and sometimes with a friend, I would go through hundreds of old magazines a night, actually buying a few when the store manager got a look in his eye, wondering if I was ever going to leave. I was finally tossed out one night when I brought my own chair.

In the late forties there were so many magazines. Most of them no longer exist, but some were particularly good. One of the lessons I learned from

them was that while many served a similar market, they all had a very distinctive look. A look that their regular customers felt at home with. A look that was carefully cultivated by their art directors.

Brodovitch at *Bazaar*, Leiberman at *Vogue*. *Life* had its characteristic style and *Look* had another. So did *Collier's* and *The Saturday Evening Post* and *This Week* and *American Weekly*. All fought for the same market, but maintained their identity. This was another asset I brought to my work. I understood the look of the magazine I was working for. This was especially important for a freelancer working on the West Coast.

I literally styled my work for a *Pageant* layout, or

her honor. Marilyn arrived from shooting at Fox Studios in a helicopter (of course), and the waiting horde was inundated by prop wash. Hats, umbrellas, sheet music, everything ended up in the pool. As the chopper landed, the photographers all rushed to be the first one there. I just stayed where I was, not wanting to be part of this to begin with, and feeling sorry that I had agreed to do it in the first place. What happened next was pure dumb luck. Marilyn headed up the stairs directly toward me. For one magic moment, I had her all to myself, and as I peered down into the viewfinder of my Rolleiflex, I could feel the hairs on the back of my neck rising. Marilyn was looking right at me, right through me! Wow! My fingers clicked off several shots, and then she was gone, pushed along by the thundering horde. But I had my photos, and I realized for the first time what all of the shouting was about.

A young Bob Willoughby with Marilyn Monroe and Ray Anthony.
Photo: Phil Stern

a *Cosmopolitan* cover. I knew *The Ladies Home Journal* never put the color green on the cover.

The other thing I did was to cut out my favorite photographs from these secondhand magazines and paste them in a big Air Force surplus photo album I had found. This honed my work, and I discovered myself pasting new and better photos over ones I'd liked a few months earlier. This helped to train my eye, and out of this melange, eventually, my own style of film coverage emerged. The point is, in all my time working with studio publicity departments, not one of them ever understood why my work was so salable while they couldn't give theirs away. They never saw the critical stylistic difference. With few exceptions, studio stills were produced in the same way as they had been from the very beginning. It was as if newspapers were the only publicity outlet.

There were always built-in problems when photographing on a sound stage. For example, when one worked on a musical, the music was always prerecorded. This was terrific, for it meant that one could photograph during the actual takes (assuming everything else was OK). However, when the sound on some of the action sequences was being recorded, something they only did once (rehearsals were usually walked through), it meant one didn't get those shots. Sometimes if people were willing after a take, one could try to recreate the sequence but it was always with less than the excitement

I came to photograph *A Star Is Born* with seven different assignments, among them *Collier's, Harper's Bazaar, Pageant, The New York Times.* But the Warner Brothers publicity office worried that I might upset Judy and hold up production. I was really keyed up, not

one felt during a take.

The same thing happened even if it wasn't action. On an emotional scene, the still men were shunted off to the side. Rehearsals had actors wearing kleenex under their chins to keep the makeup off their shirts, actresses in pincurls or in only part of their costume because the sets were so hot. It was a daily battle to bring home the material one needed. Like big game hunting, sometimes one was lucky, others not.

As a "special," I was expected always to come through, and in the course of various frustrations I devised all sorts of techniques to get the material I wanted on film.

I needed a silent camera on the set. I found an engineer in Hollywood who agreed to see if we could do that, and together we produced the first sound-blimp. It was big and clumsy, but it solved that problem...now the Jacobson blimp is found on sets all over the world.

Another problem occurred when the movie camera was put on a crane, where a still camera could not go. With my blimp and some brackets I also had designed, I was able to attach my still camera right above the lens of the motion picture camera—with the indulgence of the camera crew, of course. I had a very long release cord, but this more often than not proved to be awkward and in the way.

Jay Eyerman, a *Life* photographer, had some radio-controlled units for setting off strobe lights. I got together with him, and he adapted them to fit into the motor drive he designed for the Nikon (this was long before Nikon made a motor drive). And so we had the first radio-controlled camera. I could place it hidden, anywhere on the set or riding on the crane. It extended my coverage enormously. There were problems, but we worked them out over a period of several years.

I could never have photographed *They Shoot Horses, Don't They?* without all of this special gear. Once, in Mexico, I was shooting a *Look* layout on *Catch 22*. All of the B-25s were going to take off in close formation. We had seen previously that these gutted planes were very unsteady in the air. Taking off in close proximity to each other meant they would be in each other's prop wash.

I secured my cameras at the end of the runway, putting one very long lens to catch the crowd of planes taking off and another very wide-angle lens to shoot them as they went over. I had set both up with respective radio receivers, then beat a hasty retreat to a hill where presumably I would be safe.

The unit stillman Jack Gereghty and I were getting ready as the first wave of planes started to get airborne. I had just pushed my radio transmitter (which activates the motor-driven cameras) when Jack yelled, "Willoughby, look out!" Here was a

*U*niversal Studios hosted a charity fashion show, using their *Chalk Garden* set as background—a not-so-gentle plug for the visiting press. *Harper's Bazaar* assigned me to cover it. After the fashion show, with many of Hollywood's famous ladies as models, there

B-25 as large as life, struggling to get airborne, coming straight for me.

I dove into the dirt, as it grazed the top of my head. I started to stand up, sputtering, and spitting dirt, and he yelled at me again. Down I went again. By this time the entire airwing was gone. I had kept my finger on the transmitter button, and *Look* used the photographs. But I never saw one moment of the takeoff from my earthly embrace.

The problem of *Life* not using photographs if its film critic didn't like the film still persisted. Getting past this *Life* barrier was still uppermost in the studio's mind. As I read the script, I could almost anticipate when *Life* wouldn't be interested, so I

tried to figure other ways. It became a sort of game for me.

I convinced the *Life* fashion department to let me do a layout on the wonderful San Francisco street set built for *Flower Drum Song*. I did another fashion layout on *The Great Race*. Jack Lemmon, as the villain, always wore black. Of course, Tony Curtis, the hero, was in white. So a fashion layout for black-and-white dresses on the Tundra set, complete with a dancing polar bear, gave me the break in *Life*. The following week the film department used the big pie-fight scene. That, pardon the mixed metaphor, was the icing on the cake—a double break in *Life*. I was the hero for the day!

was dinner. As I walked past, John Gavin and his wife Cicely called me over to meet another photographer—none other than Gina Lollobrigida! She of course wanted to see my Nikkor zoom lens, and John sat me down with them and took our photo. Seeing all this fuss, some of the other photographers came over thinking they were missing something. Alas, it was only me, but one of them kindly sent me this photo with, pardon the expression, Gina holding my zoom.

Photo: Walter Fischer

It was a always great challenge, and my assignments took me to England, Scotland, Ireland, Italy, France, Austria, Switzerland, Spain, Mexico, and Venezuela. On this last location, I was covering Peter O'Toole in *Murphy's War*. I wanted to show another angle on the film, since I hadn't gotten there in time to get any sense of the plot. I hired the studio helicopter, and I flew through the jungle with Peter and his wife Sean Phillips to photograph Angel Falls. This is the world's highest waterfall, but because it is usually shrouded in clouds, very few people have ever seen it. Also, it takes days to trek to the area.

As a chopper pilot, Gilbert Chomat was well known. Working with film crews was his specialty. He flew in his bare feet to keep "the feel." A former French Air Force pilot, he was every cameraman's dream, as he would move into tight areas where others feared to tread.

Gilbert had learned from Jungle Rudi that the Venezuelan Air Force had left some aviation fuel at the midway point. It was in metal barrels and had been there for years, but Rudi figured it would be OK to use. So we were in business.

Flying over the Amazon jungle was wonderful. The birds and animals in the high trees—fantastic! With the chopper we could hover and watch scenes one could never see from the ground. Rudi had a map, but when it was time to find the falls, he confessed

"Why do you have this awful mustache, Bob?" Elizabeth asks twirling one end. I said that there was an old expression—"To kiss a man without a mustache is like eating one's food without salt!" She gave me a steely look with her violet eyes, then said, "Well, I've done very well so far on a salt-free diet." Why does one only think of a reply later? This was on *Who's Afraid of Virginia Woolf?* in 1965 at Warner Brothers Studio. Years before we'd had some good times while on location in Danville, Kentucky, for *Raintree County.* I guess

it might not be accurate. He knew how to get there, but by hiking. So by following the river we eventually found this glorious vision. After a little tour around the other tepui, where the water collects for the falls, Gilbert found Angel Falls and before we knew what he was doing, he landed the little Bell chopper right on the edge!

It was over a mile drop! Sean wouldn't look, Pete crawled over on his stomach, and I took a higher angle and photographed the scene. Gilbert saw the fog beginning to return and said, "I think we better move." We all clambered back in just as he peeled off down the side. Talk about roller coaster rides. A day or so later, Gilbert and I returned to Angel Falls for my "postcard" shots. Let me say first that

the Bell has no windows, and to get a photograph, one removes the entire side. That means the rain, wind, and general feeling of queasiness comes up to meet you all at once. Now I was looking down one mile. I tried to shoot, but as I needed to use a wide-angle lens, the rotor-blades and the skids kept getting in the way.

Gilbert, realizing this, started to ease the Bell over on its side. I'm strapped into a little lightweight bucket seat. There is no door on the side, nothing to hang on to, and I start screaming, "Wait a minute, Gilbert!" His soothing voice comes over: "Just look through your viewfinder, don't look down." Yeah, yeah, but I'm the guy hanging out of the side of the chopper! I hear the bucket seat that on anyone's list, Elizabeth was one of the most beautiful women in the world. And I danced with her all night! Danville society had turned out that night, and everyone wanted to dance with her. She begged me not to let anyone cut in. So a young fellow's dream lasted for many delicious hours as the music played on. Another time, when the director and executives suddenly flew off to MGM, leaving the cast and crew to fend for themselves, Mike Todd sent his private plane to pick up Elizabeth and bring her to Chicago. She insisted that Marguerite Lamkin, her Southern voice coach, and I join her. I had three bottles of Chateau Margaux left from a case we had miraculously discovered in Lexington, and the three of us had a picnic on the plane. These were magic moments, the sun danced through the windows and lit up her hair, her eyes... I still can't explain how I could just stare and not run for my cameras. It was too wonderful to spoil with business, I tell myself now, but what kind of photo-journalist lets an opportunity like that pass?

Photo: Mel Traxel

click as it takes the strain of my weight. A quick burst of frames from my motor drive and Gilbert eases the chopper back. I'm now beginning to wish I hadn't eaten.

I'm also beginning to regret ever coming back for a second go at this when over we go again and I get another burst out of the motor drive. Eventually I felt I had enough and motioned Gilbert to take me down to the ground. I found it nesessary to get out and walk around, to get my stomach out of my mouth, before we could go back up again and photograph the top of the tepui. It was a great adventure, I could admit later.

Part of that "special" coverage also included a visit to see the Waika tribe with Sean and Peter, which involved flying into the jungle to a dirt landing strip and boating up the Orinoco River. When we emerged from the jungle we headed for Caracas, where I called my wife Dorothy to come and meet me and we would take a trip to Peru and see Machu Picchu.

I had had some good times with Sean and Peter in Pompeii earlier, when we were filming *Goodbye Mr. Chips*, and we shared this interest in art and archeology. When Peter heard the magic name Machu Picchu, he said there was no way we could go without them. So at the spur of the moment we all joined forces and from the jungles of the Amazon, we hiked the Andes of Peru.

Eventually the press caught on to who they were, though we did have several days of blissful anonymity. Traveling with a well-known personality is often no fun. This time we were traveling with two other actors, and my Scottish wife was mistaken for a Puerto Rican actress called Sharon O'Reilly! She was even asked for autographs at the airport as Peter and Sean went off to London and I had to make a beeline first to LA to change my clothes and then the next day to Madrid to work on *The Horseman*.

Life was never dull.

By the time the family and I moved to Ireland in 1973, I had covered over 100 feature films and worked with the advertising departments of just about every major studio. At times on location, I literally created an entire ad campaign, as on *Goodbye Mr. Chips* and *Catch 22*. For twenty years my work was never out of print in the United States for even one week.

The collection of photographs in this book reflect more of the candid, behind-the-scenes material. The actual film coverage and special layouts will have to await another Willoughby book—hopefully in the near future.

Bob Willoughby
1993
Vence, France

Bob Willoughby has traveled the world as a photographer. Well known for his photographs of beautiful women and famous personalities, he became *the* specialist in covering motion pictures for the world's major magazines, his work appearing in *Life, Look, Vogue, Collier's,* and *Harper's Bazaar.*

In his long career Willoughby covered over 100 feature films, including such classics as *From Here to Eternity, A Star Is Born, The Man with the Golden Arm, Raintree County, Can Can, My Fair Lady, The Great Race, The Lion in Winter, Goodbye Mr. Chips, Catch 22, Klute,* and *The Cowboys.* During a twenty-year period Willoughby was never out of print for even a week.

His work has been exhibited in museums throughout the world. He has been awarded several gold and silver medals in international competitions, and his work is included in the collections of The National Portrait Gallery, London; The Museum of Modern Art, New York; The Bibliothèque Nationale, Paris, and Musée de la Photographie, Charleroi.

Married with four children, Willoughby now lives with his wife in the south of France. Born in Los Angeles in 1927, he studied design with Saul Bass at the Kann Institute of Art and Film at the University of Southern California. In 1974 he published *The Platinum Years* with text by Richard Schickel. *Voices from Ireland,* published in 1981, is a translation of early Irish poetry, translated by Willoughby and illustrated with his photographs of the Irish countryside. *Jazz in LA,* published in 1990, is a collector's cache of early jazz greats photographed by Willoughby in the 1950s. A series of film document books, with photographs by Willoughby, was started in 1990 and now includes *The Graduate, Who's Afraid of Virginia Woolf?, They Shoot Horses, Don't They?* and *Rosemary's Baby.*